Vegetables

Artichoke

Asparagus

Basil

Beetroot

Broad beans

Broccoli

Brussels Sprouts

Cabbage

Carrot

Cauliflower

Celery

Coriander Leaves

Cucumber

Eggplant

Green beans

Kale

Leek

Lettuce

Mushroom

Okra

Onions

Peas

Peppers

Potatoes

Radishes

Rhubarb

Spinach

Sweet Potato

Tamarind

Turnip

Zucchini

www.ingramcontent.com/pod-product-compliance
Lightning Source LLC
Chambersburg PA
CBHW050742110526
44590CB00002B/58